POEMS
of a HIDDEN
Soul

Andrea Frost

PAGE PUBLISHING
Conneaut Lake, PA

First originally published by Page Publishing 2023

ISBN 979-8-88960-131-9 (pbk)
ISBN 979-8-88960-135-7 (digital)

Library of Congress Control Number: 2023915030

Printed in the United States of America

Written in memory of my amazing band teacher, John H. Hickey (RIP—February 2005), who inspired me to always move forward. His catchphrase, "Do the Right Thing," has guided me through my paths in life.

Contents

PREFACE

In February of 2005, I was confronted with one of the biggest trag-edies of my life. My band teacher, John Hickey, died early in the morning. I will never forget walking onto campus that day. It was extra cold, and the slight breeze made it feel even colder. I walked toward the quad, and a fellow band member stopped me. We weren't the best of friends, so I was surprised they were talking to me.

"Did you hear?" His voice wavered, and I simply shook my head. "Mr. Hickey's dead."

I am sure my face looked shocked. I didn't believe him. We had been through a few schoolyard arguments before, and I didn't really trust him. I honestly thought that he was playing an exceedingly mean prank on me. I brushed past him with a mumbled "I don't believe you" and quickly headed down the steps leading to the band room. As I gripped the handle to open the door, an immense feel-ing of dread washed over me, along with the feeling of frozen metal sticking to my hand.

The room was filled with the sound of sobbing as I walked in. I could see my fellow band kids in groups, some in chairs, some in the corners of the room, but most collapsed on the floor. I looked for my closest friends and found them in the middle of the room. Quickly making my way to them, I dropped my backpack before sinking to the floor in their group. I didn't need anyone to say anything. I knew the boy from before was telling the truth now. My beloved band teacher was no longer among the living.

That day changed my perspective on a lot of different things. One of the biggest things I learned about myself was how to emo-tionally help others. I began comforting, consoling, and listening to my fellow band kids for the rest of that school year. I did not realize how much doing that took a toll on my mental health. My grades suffered, and I slipped into a pretty bad depression. Mr. Hickey was like a second father to most of the band kids, and losing him sud-denly hit us all really hard.

I found my head swimming with all kinds of negative thoughts and knew I needed to find a productive release for them. Using one of the blank notebooks I always kept on me, I decided to start writing poems. Poetry is creative, can be short, and does not always require structure or rhyming. It was the quickest, easiest, and most creative way I could express myself and the bottled-up emotions I was carrying around. I ensured anyone who wanted to read my poems knew they were just words on paper. Once the idea was written down, I no longer dwelled on it.

Like most teenagers, I wrote about all the dark stuff I could think of and loved making the things most people think are "bad" become the "good" in my poems. Reading the poems now, I can look back and chuckle at how stereotypical I could be. These poems helped me through one of the hardest parts of my life. Since then, I have fixed them up but most have remained unchanged from their original writing. I hope you enjoy them as much as I enjoyed creating them.

A Poem of the Sun

The sun is a beautiful thing
With the sparkling essence of warmth
It just sits there day in and day out
Glistening in the morning and shining in the evening
Rising and setting without a care in the world
As if the seasons never change
As if time stands still every time it shows its ever-changing face
It is the gem that will lead us to paradise
The sun is a beautiful thing

A Reflection

Bedraggled and begrudged
Cold and tempters look
A reflection of the inner self

Screaming and crying
Whining into the night
A reflection of inner feelings

Outgoing and unafraid
Energetic and happy again
A reflection of a lost hope

Quiet and hiding
Scared of tinny, little sounds
A reflection of the exposed self

Strong and brave
Not afraid to stand up
A reflection of the forgotten self

Ugly and deformed
Scaring every single thing
A reflection of the outward appearance

Beautiful and dainty
Men fall at your feet
A reflection of a lost appearance

Lost in a sea of torment
Crying and reaching out
A reflection of a tortured soul

12/01/2006

All

Blackness is overwhelming
Darkness is overcoming
Bloodiness is intoxicating
Night is what it's called

Falling deeper inside myself
Dead corpses following me down
Down to the depths of a bloodthirsty house
Demons feeding off what I used to know

Memories swimming without picture or sound
Heroes die by heroes' own hands
Villains work with villainous beings
Evil rising from death's lurking light

My body lay down
My head on the ground
No one around till morning, I'm told
Lying in the evening light, watching them dance all night

Dust seeping from my soul
Pain released from my battered shell
Sorrows bleed free on the floor
Death, my friend, has now appeared

Sleeping in the night before
Listening to the screeching of cars
People's voices ringing in my ears
All is death, and death is all

09/26/2005

All in the Mind

Breeze blowing fiercely
Tossing golden locks
Of Rumpelstiltskin's making
Time is wasting away

Lights flicker on and off
Icicle eyes glance
To and fro
Time is wasting away

Scuffle of shoes
Brushed touch of chills
A breath in the ear
Time has frozen still

A haunted whisper
Of lost souls sing
Reaching deep inside the mind
Time starts going again

Stadium lighted
Crowds roar with fear
Enemies surround me
Time their greatest fear

Battles are rising
Patience over peace
Attacking in numbers
Time will take one side

Dodging and weaving
Demons flying by
Headaches are rising
Time is flittering away

On a cold corner waiting
Wind blowing in my hair
The light turns green
Time has started to run

Hurrying across the street
Making every step count
Blending in again within the sea of feet
Time is lost to the growing noise

12/01/2006

Belief

Belief is in the mind of the believer
Whether it be for great good: God
Or a supposed great evil: Satan
Even still, some refuse to believe in any but themselves

All these kinds live among one another
Yet among them, all are some persuaders
"We are the right way. Follow us!"
All say the same; the only difference is the beliefs

Why do they argue
Are we all not the same
What is the true difference
Is there really any

What defines the differences between them
What separates all of us
Is it truly the beliefs or is it something more
Could it possibly be a blindness of possible friends

They all say that their God is the one
Then what of other's so-called God
What then does that make them
Lost, loners, or sinners

What defines someone as a sinner if they follow their own path
Can we truly define a being with that single word
Is it humane to label another
Is it faithful to your belief

03/11/2006

Bloody Melody
(Friend and Foe)

When we talk within the darkness
Then it feels like the light is gone
When the sun is finely shining
We will sing the rebel song

We have risen to the glory
Of this bloody melody
The guns fire, the cannons sing
On this field of friend and foe

When we meet in bloody battle
And the guns a firin'
We may have known one another
But in war, we're enemies

We have risen to the glory
Of this bloody melody
The guns fire, the cannons sing
On this field of friend and foe

When the night comes down upon us
We will cease the fighting then
We will lie down in our own beds
And we'll listen to the night

We have risen to the glory
Of this bloody melody
The guns fire, the cannons sing
On this field of friend and foe

The wounded lay dying
In a field of deadly fear
They wait for death to claim them
But relief isn't near

We have risen to the glory
Of this bloody melody
The guns fire, the cannons sing
On this field of friend and foe

The generals won't surrender
Their pride is just too big
The war just continues
But the battle's finally won

We have risen to the glory
Of this bloody melody
The guns fire, the cannons sing
On this field of friend and foe

Yes, we rose to that glory
Of that bloody melody
The guns fired, the cannons sang
On that field of friend and foe
On that field of friend and foe

Calling Me Away

Letting darkness fall
Writings on this wall
Figures shadowed down the hall

Haunted houses haunting
Lost, wandering spirits wanting
Just sitting here and talking

Looking at my surroundings
Old hunt calls, sounding
Going down the hall, bounding

In the end, I find you kneeling
Stock still and mortally bleeding
I see your eyes with want and needing

A new feeling now calling
Waiting, waiting for a response
Only for me to bend down, reeling

Better now than I ever was
Waiting for you to join me
Join me in a resting sleep

Now that we are together
I want to be with you forever
And stand by you through whatever

Please just don't call me away again
My soul could not take that journey again
Stop calling me away

08/18/2006

Crimson River

Drip, drip, drop
Into the river
Flip, flip, flop
Out on the land

White marrow rocks
Line the banks
Powder-bone sandbags
Along the way

Life-giving life leaving
Donate again
Sharp objects contribute
To its continuing growth

Let it flow
Free and fast
Let it have its space
A mile between each place

Can't use a boat
Can't use a raft
Can't float above it
Can't sink below

Watching it go
On and on
To the beat of your heart
To wrists of crimson river

05/16/2006

Crown of Death

Singing in the darkness
Lurking in the shadows
Missing in the crowds
Working like the crows
The crown of death is existing

Living in despair
Breathing in rotted air
Lying in bone marrow's dust
Sleeping in a grave's rotted hole
The crown of death is traveling

Dead in my crimson heart
Suffocating in my ribs, sharp spears
Falling into death's warm embrace
Working in God's cold, fading light
The crown of death is closer

Deep in spaces freezing baron void
Far inside my hating being
Close to what bright life does fear
Shallow waters of life now exist
The crown of death is coming

Stalking the reassesses of death
Hunting in death's rotting crimson forest
Waiting for the colors to finally drain
Crying a crimson blood river
The crown of death is here

09/08/2005

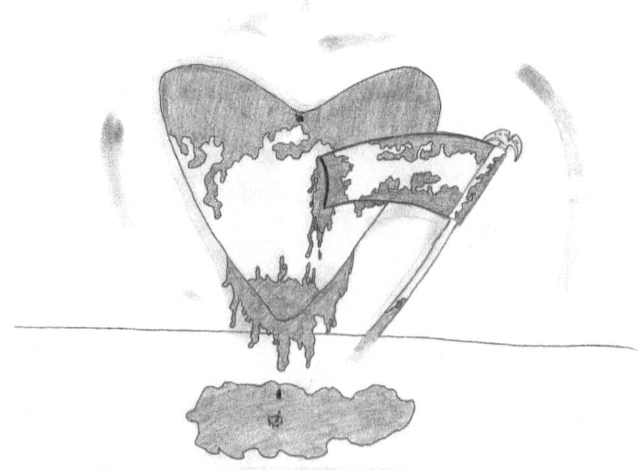

Dark Love

Voices deep inside of me
Telling me to kill the soul
Winning at gaining new blood

Voice is willing me to claim
Claim the man it wants
Claim the soul it craves

Lust in my eyes
The killing intent is there
Both are overwhelming my peace

Oriented and alone
Cold and distantly far
Lost and wandering where

Questions release
Quietness unreal
Quickness, quiet, and unquestionable

Understanding evil beliefs
Losing the light of the beyond
Reddish flames burning my holy side

Dark, hidden love lost
No matter how I try
My dark love is lost to a thing

Losing the affection
Chills my very soul
Hell's fire is burning out

I drain the blood to lose
I regain the soul once lost
I leave myself behind

Demon in my head
Calling to the dead
Let me fall to death

Letting reality take over
I lose my strength to continue
The dark love I lust for lost

He is there in my grasp
But already in another's
I lost to that thing

Fighting, I will no longer continue
Waiting out the inevitable
Patiently praying on the dark love

My hating dark love
Lost to a weak darkness
The only thing left of my soul

Is my dark, haunting love

11/07/2005

Deliverance

Doth the future do you see
Yoth child born of flames
Ye soul of sight hath see him here
Round yonder Bustrack tree
He prances, and he dances
With blades of burning bark
Bark of which grows heavy with ye heart
Yer heart of which with crystal ice
Doth burn his dusty hand
A hand which on many moons hath ended mortal lives
'Tis lives of old and lives of new
Hath succumbed to his bloody bark blade
And though ye may be calm
When faced with a boney face
Yer spirit will fall victim
To his sweet words of wishes
His voice which sounds like lust incarnate
Do not fight and do not resist
For yer fate will be worse than death
Yer fate all depends on your spirit's strength
Stare him down, attempt to escape
Ending in failure fare
He will whisper to you in night's early light
Whisper words of laughter and sin
His words, like drugs, will reel you in
Arms open wide to accept you
Blade poised and ready to strike
Standing tall and strong and proud
Awaiting you, yer soul, yer bleeding heart

09/14/2006

Demons at My Door

No one here
But yet I fear
The silence from within

I know they are there
Just outside
Waiting by the door

I wish to know
And not to hide
From what I know is inside

I know who they are
But still, I fall
Afraid of the silence from within

Songs sing inside my skull
Beckoning me to join the dead
I lift my head, and now I see them

They are at the door
Waiting to be asked in
As I call, they come to me

They help me to come back home
They are not evil as believed
They all help me and become one with me
They are the demons at my door

05/11/2005

Drama

Everyone around me
So carefree and happy
Masked by fake love
And burning desire

Slime like the human race
Needs to burn in the
Blinding light of
Heaven

The place they all
Want to go to
Let them have it
I will take hell

My comfort place
When I am ill
Alone and in need
I wish to go there

Warmth and caring
Kindness and slaving
Torture my brain
Hell is my comfort zone

05/05/2006

Dreaming

Silver liquid burning me
Drowning me and killing me
Darkness lifting up the air
Suffocating the silver flare

Wrinkles slowing down my breath
Intoxicating electricity
Burning spirits of the dead
Liquid flowing from their bed

Belief fading from fantasy
Falsifying the truth and reality
Bleeding home and further
Dawning in the midnight day

Breathing down my placid back
Breaking, breathing, bleeding black
Lurching, turning, yearning hate
Deathly lusting after fake fantasy

Talking with death
Discussing suicidal motivation
What is to become of me
Bleeding in that spot

Wantingly asking to be released
Lustfully looking at death
Believing in life being gone
Never even opening my eyes
Dreaming of murderous times

10/31/2005

Drowned in Me

Running river
Rising higher and higher
Never known to stop
Never known to wait

Pulling stronger
Can't last any longer
Let me go within
Drowning deeper with me

Lesson learned
Teacher had taught
Though never believed
The river a killer indeed

Let my hand go
The pulse of life gone
My new pulse revealed
In the land of the dead

Coming back
To talk with you
Only to find you
With someone new

You say you love them
You told me so too
You were the one to drown me
Now you drowned in me

08/10/2006

Eat of My Fill

Rotting corpses
Of burning flesh
Staleness of death
Stench of the deceased

Carvings so perfect
Each equal in size
Cooking slowly
Roasting the lifeless taste

Basted in sauce
That makes everyone starve
Lost in a graveyard
Of boiling stew

Too many spices
Makes the meal all too hot
Let it sit and get cooler
Helped by death's cold touch

Perfect temperature
To eat now
Serve it to us
Give equal portions to all

We wait for the last one
To sit next to me
I swear on this dead meal
To eat of my fill

08/10/2006

Eternal Rest

Lying on the floor, I cry
Crimson tears of death
Screaming at the tears I made
Falling deeper, deeper inside

The decomposing flesh I have
Is slowly falling away
Eyes made up from my pain
Pools of death is my beating heart

Living in the mortal world
Where I must always hide
Wishing for a better home
Where I can die alone

People, places, things, and times
All unknown and all around me
Waiting for an unhappy thing
Death, my friend, has gone again

My tears become spears
My heart, a waiting bomb
Time is of the essence here
Life a newfound game

Crying, crying crimson
Going, going home again
Crimson tears of death
Deliver me to my eternal rest

06/01/2005

Existence

It's cold outside
The sun is gone
I wonder why
Why do we exist

The light of life is faint
A shadow overhead
It has not come to pass yet
The shadow has yet to arrive

I wish to know the shadow
A sign for what is to come
The light that will extinguish
What little existence that still fights

I will help the shadow
I will sing its song
It will be my friend
It will entwine with me

The shadow is what has yet to come
It knows what is needed for us to live
It can help or it can hurt
And it can kill and destroy us all

The shadow is a savior
The shadow is a killer
The shadow does not exist yet
The shadow is me and my existence

05/17/2005

Existence II

It's cold outside
The sun is gone
I wonder why
Why in heaven's name
Why do we exist

The light of life is faint
A shadow overhead
It has not come to pass yet
The shadow has yet to arrive
The darkness still lingers oh so far away

I wish to know the shadow
A sign for what is to come
The light that will extinguish
What little existence still fights
What little time we have

I will help the shadow
I will sing its song
It will be my friend
I will be its body
It will combine with me

The shadow is what has yet to come
It knows what is needed for us to live
It can help, or it can hurt
And it can kill and destroy us all
Or will it be the savior we all are waiting for

The shadow is a savior
The shadow is a killer
The shadow does not exist yet
The shadow now has a host
The shadow is me and my existence

05/17/2005

Explanation

Life can be an everlasting time
Love can be an everlasting thing
Life is as real as love's sight
Love is as real as life's feeling

Life can be a deadly feeling
Love can be a hateful sight
Kill both life and love
Live both death and hate

Death can be an ensuing time
Hate can be an endowing thing
Death is as real as hate's thought
Hate is as real as death's touch

Death can be a lifelong feeling
Hate can be a loving sight
Let the hate consume you
Feel death's loving touch

Death and hate are waiting
Life and love are far behind
Living in death's house
Feeling the love from someone's hate

Life and death
Love and hate
All are feelings and states
None explains anything

07/14/2005

Fight for Freedom

Brothers and sisters
Cousins and uncles
Fathers and mothers
Daughters and sons

Fighting and dying for you

Planes flying faster
Rising to a challenge
Crashing, burning
Evil intentions fulfilling

Others weeping and giving to you

Inspirational speeches
Chaos follows its wake
People are screaming
Anger at the challenge to freedom

We will go and help with you

Patience is waning
Haters show up
Security increases
Homeland will stay safe

Sleep in your bed
Silently dream
While all us over here
Fight to keep you free

09/11/2006

Freedom

Freedom does not come free
Though most believe that it is
Freedom is not free for me or you alike
We must fight and bleed, cry and see
Freedom does not come free

Freedom Fighters

Darkness cascading
Light is fading
Blood of life waning
Souls lined up waiting

Debating next course of action
World just sitting there laughing
Brother's sisters now accusing
Mistakes, conspiracies, all just confusing

Send out my boys
Let them earn their keep
USMC marches down our street
LAVs line the streets

No one to help them
Except their brothers-in-arms
Some go out the heroes
Others are never called

Oppressed people calling for help
Our free spirits answer
Fireworks, blasts, kaboom
Our light show against you

No matter the price
No matter the place
We will defend our homeland
Because freedom doesn't come free

09/11/2006

Friend

A friend is a person who is always there for you
A friend is like family, loving and kind
A good friend will never betray you
A friend is like an everlasting jawbreaker; you savor it forever
A friend is like an angel, a savior to your soul
A friend is whatever we believe them to be
As their friends, we must live up to the other's expectations

God

The death of a savior, the life of our king
Through love and pain, we were born
The light of a star shown brighter than morn
He sacrificed here for us
Live, Lord Jesus Christ

Graduation

Boring lectures
Tiresome work
Pissed off teachers
And a social mess

Wake up early
Go to bed late
Try not to sleep
In the middle of class

Four years of torture
After eight years before
Two to four years yet to come
All for one moment in time

Walk down the aisle
Move the tassel halfway
Walk up some stairs
Flashes light your eyes

Get a small paper
Shake hands with "the man"
Smile at the camera
Walk away just as you came

This one little paper
The fruit of your toils
This one slip of paper finalizes your
Graduation

05/15/2006

Halloween

Trick-or-treating, candy-eating
Sneaking, scaring, monster-tarring
Little kitties, candy-snatching
Lanterns lighting, jack-o'-lanting

Darkened skies and lightning strikes
Thunder roaring, mountain soaring
Haunting housing, scary spooking
Flying further, laughing faster

Ohh and awing
Eek and acking
Jumping and laughing
Spooking and splashing

Stuffing and snacking
Leaping and snatching
Fighting and screaming

Candy sweetening
Booby trap laying
Hiding out with creepy masks
Dead are walking with past movie stars

The devil arrives
Monsters are born
Witches do live
Ghosts come out to play

All these and more
Happen on all hallows eve

10/31/2005

  Andrea Frost

Hateful Devotion

I'm turning in my grave
Slipping the pills to my man
Not waiting for redemption
I slit the repressive throat

Cursing my abominable fate
Fleetingly calling to a crumbled soul
Finally feeling resentment of you
Screw someone else's life up

Needing to bleed my anger
Taking the knife again
Needing to still my sorrow
Taking the pain again

Listening to your lies
Trying to revise
Lifting you of fears
Taking in the numb

Waking to find you gone
Walking to bring you home
Wanting to take a breath
Willing to go the steps

A path of unbridled hatred
A plan of mysterious pain
A knowledge of burning sensations
A life of undying devotion

02/03/2006

Hellp

Lying in wait for death to come
Love is gone; life is empty
Lying next to you, I cry
Hellp me to see the fire

Life is invisible; life is impossible
Love is a useless thing
Wait till I leave again
Hellp is on the way

Walking down a hallway
Singing to death a song about hell
Lying in wait for fires to burn
Hellp me to see the darkness

Life is invisible; life is impossible
Love is a useless feeling
Wait till I leave again
Hellp is on the way

Leaping and screaming, I die
Down to the depths of hell
Walking down the river of blood
Hellp me to fly to freedom

Life is invisible; life is unmeaning
Hate is a helpful thing
Wait till I leave again
Hellp has come too late

Lying in a pool of blood
I have just drowned again
Take me to hell again
Hellp never came

Life is invisible; life is forgettable
Hate is a loving thing
Now I am left alone
Hellp is never the same

How I Died

How I died. Now there is a question.
Well I will tell you how I died.
I lived but two days ago, and I'll tell you now I did not die
    very slow.
There was a kid looking at me, and he said just two words:
    "Godspeed."
I looked at him and asked him who he was.
He said to me, "I'm an angel waiting for you."
He asked me to stay and wait
For he knew what to do.
Right before noon, a gun went off and a bullet hit.
I fell to the floor but did not die quick.
Later on, I heard someone call, "Come, my child."
I looked up, and there he was.
I said, "God, please don't let me die before my son has his first birthday."
He looked at me, then looked right at the boy.
The boy said one more time, "I am an angel waiting for you."
And now you know that "I am an angel waiting for you."

Hunts

Death, a love
Forever lost
Life, a killer
Haunting me

I want it to end
I want to be free
No longer a slave
To life's light

Wanting my love
Fearing my hunter
Pull love toward me
Fling away the hunter

Worship no one or thing
Believe in only my beliefs
Death as my forever lover
And life as my eternal hunter

Breath loves perfume
Suffocate the hunter's lungs
Bathing lover's liquid
Scream at the hunter's thought

Death, my love
Life, my hunter
Love hunts my hunter
Hunter hunts my love

04/01/2006

Lasting Plea

Walking down the darkened path
Letting spill my plea
Understanding shadowed life
Killing the inside of me

Letting go my painful cries
Making horror sound
Leaving all the innocents
Bleeding straight to the ground

Begging for my final release
Wishing all the way
Panting in this open hall
Blood, the path to hell

All the essence of evil light
Absorbed with fierce delight
Telling in the hollow halls
Screaming to be set free

Life, evaporating in my hand
Hardening in crusting blood
Bleeding from newfound wounds
Patiently waiting for a cold sensation

Death, so appealing to subconscious mind
Wanting to be welcomed in
Waiting for the pain to fade
Death, my lasting plea

02/20/2006

Life and Death

Life is made up of fun and joy to me
But most people fear death
I don't for I believe that death is a new journey for us to lead
Death may come suddenly, slowly, quietly
Life is loud, furious, and fast
Life is not as fun as death for death is life in a new light

Life-Giving Light

Sleeping peacefully, waiting for the light
Dawn is fast approaching
Heaven's coming light

The skies outside are now slightly shining
The waking of Apollo now has begun
Racing across the heavens comes a chariot of gold

Singing alleluia to the coming light
Rejoicing at the coming of the dawn's life-giving light
Light of life comes forth to us with everlasting love

Sing to us, O Living Light
We all need your love
We all care for your life

Life is love in a heavenly way
Love is life to a beating heart
Light is life and love in everyone's seeing heart

Light Shine Down

Shining in the light above
Like heaven's grinning grace
A roselike petal falls to its place
On God's living earth

The earth rumbles, hungry for the sun
Mountains climb, climb, climb
As the birds twit, twit, twit
And the sun glitters, glitters, glitters

Mountains high and mountains low
Whisper his name to all
Shadows crawl away and hide
At dawn's coming light

Birds sing, bees buzz
Everything's all right
Light shines, night becomes day
Listen to what I say

07/28/2005

Live and Love

Live and love
Or
Love and live

Either way, you will be free
A life of love is full of happiness
And love will bring all a wonderful life
So, of course, it is better
To have loved and lost than to never have loved at all

Lonely Places

Bony cup of paling death
Decaying dust of timely demises
Bloated faith of fading faces
Icy touch of soulless breath

Calming breeze of putrid sight
Trifling ruffle of blood-lined evidence
Humorous sneer of captive bones
Purified linins of a demon's touch

Light coins of sinful endeavors
Whispered song of fallen angels sing
Black prison of satin lining brings
Cold coverings of true mother's mirth

Screeching talk of lighted faces
Drowning eyes of shadowed figures
Mournful humming of alighted tunes
Pure white bed of bloodstained steel

Hateful calling of forgotten voices
Blank mind of remembered pasts
Draining colors of artful masterpieces
Soundless sleep of restless souls

Heavy lid of constricting wood
Concrete walls of natural making
Infested vest of animals creating
Lonely places of untrusting faces

11/29/2006

Love Is Lost

Lost love makes you stronger
Keeping love gives you a weakness as well as strength
Love and lose the fire few
The next is not far behind
Love and keep
Your life is complete
Never love at all and you will be empty all the time

Man at My Door

He stands there
So quiet and still
His hands are as cold
Cold as Northern ice

Squinting blankly into space
Staring quietly at my heart
His glistening red eyes bore down on me
Promising death if I speak one word

His left arm is nothing but, but
A mangle mess of muscles, veins, and bones
Dangling not but an inch was left
So loose you could just tap it and watch it fall

His evil smirk is bloody
His glare so intense it hurts
Like holy water on the throat
Death he has surpassed

He wants me to help him
He does fear something
But I fear him
His arm, his eyes, his smirk

He is the man at my door
That dark and evil spirit
That lurks just outside
My fragile sliding glass door

10/08/2005

Monster

As time ticks, ticks, ticks away
And the summer sun sets again
As years go by, a summer again gone
Another life slipping, dwindling away
As days turn to nights and dawns to dusks
A creature shall appear to you who does not heed
A hunter who hunts all that is near
A human who was chosen and spit upon
A person whose luck is not with them
Again, night turns to day and dusk to dawn
A child who is hungry and tired
A hindered voice that shall never cry
A humbled individual who needs all's help
A prisoner of themselves and of society
Although this life is hard and sad
Although they might be frightened and feared
A day of sneaking, hunting, and murdering
A job of the assassin will cast aside all emotions
A night of stalking, hating, and massacring
A life of the devil's beast will become an unknown legend and destiny
Altogether, their life is of the devils
Altogether, their time is never far-off
As they die, they rise again
All their evil will stay in the world
All the people know, but they do not speak
A child being called many names
A name that all do not know
A name that she herself has unwilfully chosen
Angel, Devil, Dragon, Demon, Evil, Death, and Monster

09/02/2005

Murderous Night

Fading in the darkness
My breath is very thin
Please understand that
Your life is mine

Killing all the people
Filling them with pain
Belief is never wavering
Let the pain begin

Light, it strangely burns me
Lets me shake with glee
Murderous night cascading
Letting me become free

Tightening up my mind
Loosening up my heart
Stabbing at you lightly
Taking every breath

Light, it strangely burns me
Lets me shake with glee
Murderous night cascading
Letting me become free

Murdering every soul
Suffocating every breath
Flattening out your chest
Beating you to death

Lightning, thunder sounding
Storm's mighty breath
Bringing wrath upon me
Cleaning up the mess

Light, it strangely burns me
Lets me shake with glee
Murderous night cascading
Letting me become free

11/03/2005

Murderous Side

Crumbling beneath you
My soul cannot rest

Seething in hatred
My bones have been crushed

Tortured in darkness
My soul rests in fire

Breathing within me
My death shall not speak

Open your eyes
Don't you see how I die

Open the walkway
To hell's burning flame

All stay in hatred
All shall be touched
Running its burning
Fingers on me

Crumbling, seething, needing you

Hatred unstirred
Death's only touch

Burning delight in this hellish facade

Water not running nor can it stay
All the good things have now burned away

All stay in hatred
All shall be touched
Running its burning
Fingers on me

Tracing my soul
Begging to die

Looking right at me
Eyes cursed by fire

Talking with screams

All stay in hatred
All shall be touched
Running its burning
Fingers on me

Running from darkness
Curled shall it be

Waiting for calming sensation
Of death

Now are you listening
Now can you hear

I call upon you
By mass genocide

All stay in hatred
All shall be touched
Running its burning
Fingers on me

This is my call
This is my call

This is my call
To your murderous side

All stay in hatred
All shall be touched
Running its burning
Fingers on me

All stay with the devil
All shall be tortured
Running its burning
Scalpels on me

All stay in hell and
All shall be turned
Bringing its burden
Straight onto me

All stay in oppression
All shall be killed
Racking its freezing
Skeleton on me

This is the call for mass genocide
All to your murderous side

01/30/2006

My Body

Small and dainty
Deadly and strong
Scraggly and scrawny
Perfect as an angel

Despised by none
Envied by some
Loved by all
Curses shall befall

Gold dust bestowed
Time never ages
Suffocating love
Faintly afraid

Love versus hate
Fear versus courage
Existence versus nonexistence
Heaven versus hell

Scared but not afraid
Hot but never warm
Tired but cannot sleep
Awake but thy eyes will not open

No one denies it
For curses shall follow
Those who betray it
Die in sorrow

Life cannot contain it
Death too small to hold it
Love can never touch it
Hate shall never taint it

It has influenced some
Love distilled from others
Sorrow flows from it
Hatred bearing on some

Since all these is written
And still, no one has seen it
All I ask of you is to look at
My body

06/14/2005

My Name

Alone and afraid
Quiet and sad
Silent as death
Left by thy self

Called out by none
Whispered by some
Feared by all
Curses shall befall

Dust in the wind
A whisper of time
Tainted by hate
Faintly alive

Love versus hate
Fear versus courage
Life versus death
Time versus human

Scared yet not afraid
Cold yet never cool
Tired yet cannot sleep
Awake yet thy eyes never open

No one dared speak it
For curses will follow
Those who whisper it
Die in sorrow

Life cannot contain it
Death too small to hold it
Love can never catch it
Hate will never taint it

It has influenced some
Fear distilled from others
Kindness flows from it
Hatred bearing toward it

Since all these is said
And still, no one has spoken it
All I ask of you is to say
My name

06/14/2005

Night Is the End of All

Night is dark and dead
Night is free and calm
Night is what I love
Night is what I fear

Darkness is the key
Hell is the lock
Night is the chest
Death is the prize

Night is time for sleep to come
But never does it find me
I wonder down the hallways
Fires on both sides

Life is falling before me
Yet I never die
I wish for death to claim me
But still, the reaper isn't here

Night is the cause of this
I shouldn't have opened the door
Darkness was the key for me
Death my lasting prize

Death is an everlasting gift
Hell is a destiny never fulfilled
Darkness a world above all others
Night is the end of all

04/11/2005

Prayer

Silent plea of silent words
Hands are folded in begging form
Minds at rest with falsified peace

Bleeding hands and feet
Fake love to comfort you
What is this

Prayer

Dried tears of "heavens" keep
Boring sights of bushes flame
Stone laws born to us

Trust betrayed for worshipped gold
Anger broke a mountain of old
What can this be

Ten Commandments

Following these laws
Believed in unfaithful comfort
Begging to those above

Talking about your futile wants
Wishing for futile dreams
Believing in unreal miracles

Prayer

03/26/2006

Rayo

She sits alone
On a rock way out there
No one alive around her
Still death surrounds her

Breathing death's stench
Like an expensive perfume
Glittering eyes of hate
Glaring at the bones

Wanting life but losing
Being free with chains
Bones of dead are glowing
Singing songs of life

05/12/2005

Reborn

Silence seeping through the shield
Of pain and horror bring
Lightning strikes of burning sins
Thunder rolls off putrid howls

Breathing roughly beneath the skin
Fire erupting and burning in
Cinders falling with snowflake grace
Laying a blanket of dusty death

Flames licking near the floor
Becoming the burning souls
Evil kissing up the rail
Climbing to the head

Brushing off the cinders
Lighting with a fearful light
Shimmering with hateful mirth
Blinking back the heat

Wishing for agony
Release from plentiful pain
Wanting a nice release from here
Flames lapping at my core

Fire burned down, and ashes die out
Egg born of fire light up the night
Cracking in heat, head poking out
Pheonix reborn in evening light

02/20/2006

Say

I truly am alone
Haltered all around
Why do people shun me
Throw me down and hunt me

Life is draining from my soul
Calming cold consumes me
Water flowing from my veins
Red wine turns black in front of me

Foreboding answers still allude
Waiting for the timeless sing
Black and blue, red and dead
Soulless letting up

Belief is never helping
Fear is calming nerves
This is what I search for
This is what I want
Here is what I say

10/08/2005

Silver Conciseness

Silver flames ignite
Consumes in fear's delight
Sharp claws pawing at the door
Conciseness is burning away

Silver fangs gleaming
Drenching flesh in suffocating suicide
Delivering hellish flame
Conciseness is drowning away

Silver eyes piercing
Slurping up my tainted soul
Deriving breath from my inflamed chest
Conciseness is dwindling away

Silver lips screaming
Burdening me with secretive lies
Drowning my mind in the world's torment
Conciseness is flying away

Silver hair constriction
Surrounding my porcelain neck
Caressing my frozen cheek yet I can't touch it
Conciseness is blurring away

Silver sanity reflecting
Releasing all my memories
Revitalizing my darkened insanity
Conciseness is now bleeding away

10/18/2005

   Andrea Frost

Sleep

Drooping and heavy
My eyes wish to close

Weak and trembling
My body will buckle soon

Numb and unfeeling
My legs refuse to run

Small and powerful
My arms ready to fight

Long and limber
My hands work their magic

Slow and sloth like
My mind can't comprehend

Blurry and unfocused
My awareness dwindles

Frozen but warm
My heart beats for me

Quiet and undone
My voice refuses to sing

Lost and lonely
My soul wishes for sleep

12/01/2006

Son

I wish to know and not to hide
From the shadow's screeching, screaming
From the depths of hell once came
Searching for my mother's son

Death is afraid of the light
Night is all my life and love and happiness
Don't let the light steal it away
My mother's son is dead

07/27/2005

Sun

Sun, sun, go away
Let the moon
Come out and play

Always dusk
And never dawn
In the earth's wide sky

09/10/2005

Tails

Flying through the room
Evil flying doom
Letting evil boom

Long and fast
Sleek and strong
Hard and sharp

Reaching from my hands
Blinding all my fans
Slashing from my hands

Moving as if alive
Water, fire, air, earth
Elements of old
Dark, light, life, death, purity, and hate
Elements of new

Lashing fiercely at you
Tearing out your soul
Bringing it to me

Absorbing what I claimed
Power starts to flow
Fires burn inside

Taking on a new form
Splitting and shaping anew
Letting black fires calm them
They are my ten devil tails

11/08/2005

Tainted

Scraping at the entrance
No door willingly gives way
Forcing down the head that screams
Silence never destroyed

Evil lurking just below
Dark blackness conceals the evil's existence
I struggle on the damp grass
Chills travel down my spine

Something slimy hits my cold, bare abdomen
A sinister wind blows and chills my very bone
I shiver as the evil things trace my body
Touching my porcelain, pale skin, tainting me

The evil from down below jabs painfully at me
The more I struggle, the more it hurts
As the vice grips my throat
Drowning my pitiful pleas for help

My abdomen tightened unwillingly
The evil slowly backing away
But my luck was not with me this night
As it keeps returning, leaving, and returning again

The vices cycle never seems to quell
As evil just keeps reaching in
All I see now is something black and smooth
Its evil grips the trigger and rings death's bell
Now I sleep in eternal darkness with
Tainted body, bone, and blood

09/19/2005

Taking

Sleep is overtaking me
Eyelids drooping down
Water slowly trickling
The fever finally quelled

Slowly looking up again
I see his face shinning back at me
Though the water seemingly fled
A tidal wave does soon appear

Dropping down to the floor
Water droplets rain on to the carped ocean
Falling to my knees
As if I was a lone samurai in my final battle

Surrounded by emotional faces
My frown disappears
My face and body become stiff and still
All sounds have ceased

Time slows and darkens
I am alone in a black abyss
No sound permits, no light reviles, no life exists
I am a stone with water flowing freely

As I come to see him again
He is smiling happily with me
The picture then fades
Taking with it my human sanity
Taking with it my emotional mask of feat
Taking with it me

11/08/2005

The Light

I sit alone, and I pray to be noticed
I wish to see the light
Someday soon
I need to be held by someone who sees
I wish to see the light

My only wish will never be
I shall never be seen
They walk right by
Never seeing me
I'm alone in a desert of grief

I wish to see the light
Someday soon
I need to be held by someone who sees
I wish to see the light

They walk straight past
Giving not but sand to me
Why, oh, why, do you shun me so
Always leaving me alone
I won't survive on my own

I wish to see the light
Someday soon
I need to be held by someone who sees
I wish to see the light

Looking up, I see the stars
The lonely and distant stars
So far, far away

But yet, in my mind, I can touch their fiery light
I can hear them calling, saying
"Come, come to be one with us"
"Come, come to be one with us"

I wish to see the light
Someday soon
I need to be held by someone who sees
I wish to see the light

My mother used to say
"The stars are lost souls comforting one another"
I loved my mother, but she left me here
In this desert of self-pity

I know what to do, but will I do it or
Will someone come and embrace me
Will I see the light, oh, will I see the light
Someday soon

04/29/2005–05/16/2006

The Night of Dreams

I lay in bed
A peaceful sleep
My mind is working, turning, spinning
All the time I'm swirling, whirling, learning

In the back, I see a light
A bright and fiery light
But still a dark cloud is overhead
Night and dreams come to be one

I see them all
I truly do
I see all beams
And at all nights

Dreams of dreams
Nights of nights
Dreams of nights
Night of dreams

All are here
All are gone
I see nothing
I see all

I wish to be
I am not here
Am I a dream?
Or
Is a dream me?

The Shadow on the Wall

I stand alone
No one around
Looking down
I see no sound
I hear no heartbeat

I look around
Death is here
An all around
I wish to speak
But not a peep will be heard

A song is heard
No one around
I wish to be heard
But nothing is to be found
I am alone

I look at the wall right across from me
Life is not something to fear
So now standing silently still and alone
I look up to see shining down angrily on me

A mirror is smirking not that far from me, reflecting back a broken soul
I turn around to look behind
And I find a shadow solemnly, desperately, angrily, painfully looking
    back at me
All I am and all I was is quietly the shadow on the wall

04/11/2005

The Shadow on the Wall II

I stand alone
No one around
Looking down
I see no sound
I hear no heartbeat

I look around
Death is here
And it is surrounding me
I wish to speak and talk to you
Lying on the darkened ground
But not a peep will be heard by you nor me

Soon a song I finally hear
But still no one is near
I truly wish to be heard
But nothing, nothing is to be found on this ground
I am truly left alone

I look at the tainted wall
As bloody arms reach for me
Life has nothing to be afraid of
Nothing, that is, except death
Now in this deadly hall, I stand still and alone
Looking up I see shining angrily down on me
A mirror

Smirking not that far from here
Reflecting back a dead and broken soul
Turning to see what is left behind me
I find a shadow solemnly, depressingly, angrily
Painfully looking back at me

Now I know
Though no one spoke a word
Sitting here on this blood-soaked wall
Waiting for some sort of call
Just sitting here on this thirsty wall

Bending now to take a look
The ceiling starts to fall
Looking once again down this haunted hall
There I see the blood-burned barriers
Crying in these haunted hall walls
Still just sit here on this tainted wall

In the mirror, I look once more
Carrying in this place
Finally, looking at myself, blackened bones and
Bloody bodies near
Everything I now know

All I am and all I was
On this haunted hallway
Was the quiet shadow on a bloodied wall

07/21/2005

The Son of Man

Believing in the spirit
Living in the blood
Flowing in the body

Metallic as the moon
Heavy as our hate
Cold as a burning hell

Pain beginning once again
Love slowly fading
The Son of God is dead

Seeking out what I crave
Hunting down the Lord
Waiting for the time to come

Souls haunt my burning ears
Evil lurking in the shadows
Life is lost and dead
The Son of Man is dead

10/08/2005

The Wall

Talking to a wall
A happy wall of mine
One that is not stained
One that shines and shines

I give this wall my secrets
For it will never tell

Though you may think me crazy
I really couldn't care
You are the kind of person
That put my nice wall there

Although my wall has sisters
I don't like them as much

One of them is similar
With a black dot upon its cheek
She is marred with an evil stain
That sister is a sinner

Another seems to cry
With red tears of rain
They run down in rivulets
This sister always feel pain

The last sister is an oddball
She has a hole cutout
But something locked it up
She is a secretive sister indeed

Still unlike the others
I like my sister best

   Andrea Frost

She is pure and clean
Not a single mark can be seen
She is neither sad nor mean
My sister is the nicest

She listens to my tails
Never does she retort to any of my thoughts

She only sits and listens
She is always quiet and calm
Once she did weep
But of water not of blood

She wept for me
And not herself

She was sad for me
For when the monsters came
Who stole her pure, pure color
And put this evil thing on me

No longer can I move freely
Only talk and mumble clearly
She wept for me but that's okay
Because though I have no movement

I will always, always
Have my sister wall

12/01/2006

Thoughts

Blackened flames of hindered death
Wondering souls of spirit's flesh
Stunning knives of stinging bow
Lighted lamp of peaceful glow

Existents gone of life repent
Severed hearts of hatreds hearth
Burning cinders of forgiving souls
Ravens flight of winged tears

Lessened hope of darkened rooms
Pitch-black lights of hope shall bloom
Lifelong ventures of burning swings
Childs laugh of puttered sings

Lifted heart of bed rail's flame
Sacred heart of scandals song
Lifelong wish of breathing brings
Longing death of living beings

Whispers haunt of coldness bares
Hardened eyes of ice cold lies
Dancing flames of wasted strife
Begging burns of heartfelt cries

Lifting cold of hardness gone
Wanted pain of healing's kind
Loved ones lost of burdens bare
Tainted thoughts of murders be

03/11/2006

Time

Ticktock, ticktock
Time
Ticktock, ticktock
Time
Ticktock, tick…

Time, *tock*, time, *tick*, time, *tock*
Time, time, time, *cuckoo, cuckoo, cuckoo*

Waiting here by the clock
Cuckoo, cuckoo, cuckoo
Waiting, waiting
Cuckoo, cuckoo
All alone, left to die
Time, time
Die time, die time
Cuckoo, cuckoo

Left all alone in an empty room
No matter what the time turns, never free
Watched by the one who used to love
Left all alone with no one else around

Time never waivers no matter what
Time, by the hour, passes by
Cuckoo, cuckoo, cuckoo

Time is the enemy, time is the foe
Letting me wither away, away, away
Letting me slowly be forgotten
Keeping me forever just to be locked inside

Time never waivers no matter who
Time, by the minute, passes by
Cuckoo, cuckoo, cuckoo

Release me from your grasping hands
Let my pleas go free, free, free
Leaving me with no one no matter who they are
Let me just be left alone forever

Time never wavers no matter when
Time, by the second, passes by
Cuckoo, cuckoo, cuckoo

I'm not that important, neither you nor no one else
Leave me weak and searching for you
Help you never give; now I beg for you to be here
Help me to fight the master time

All alone left to die
Time, time
Die time, die time
Cuckoo, cuckoo
Waiting here by the clock
Cuckoo, cuckoo, cuckoo
Waiting, waiting
Cuckoo, cuckoo

Time, time, time
Cuckoo, cuckoo, cuckoo
Time, *tock*, time, *tick*, time, *tock*

Ticktock, tick
Time
Ticktock, tick

Time
Ticktock, ticktock
Cuckoo, cuckoo, cuckoo

05/11/2006

Watching the World

The night is young
The stars are out
The moon is shining
Eerily watching the world

It sits there stationary
Only moving with the tides
And the turning of this land
Forever watching the world

Songs have been written
Of the snow-white globe
Moods have been felt with its intent
But he is always watching the world

No matter the time
No matter the place
Wherever you are
She is silently watching the world

It may have a face
Of woman or man
But it still will be seen
Sightlessly watching the world

Hanging in the sky
Be bright blue or black
Never leaving our side
Continuously watching the world

12/01/2006

Will

Standing on a corner
Very scantily dressed
Watching as the cars go by
Hungry eyes always watching

Wolf, cat, and "hey, babe" calls
Surrounding the air breathed in
Body shivering in the street
Shaking in the breeze

Walking on the paved highway
Alone and silence unbroken
Dirty hair whipping at my face
As if to try and tame me

Buyers all looking, searching, yearning
Body's not but just their toy
Money flying in the wind
Liquor, drugs, control this place

Coming up upon a place
Burning screams echo
Sleeping in tattered sheets
Being strangled by unreturned love

Money is the powerhouse
Controlling all my life
Money may be what buys my body
But never can it contain my will

11/28/2005

About the Author

Andrea was born and raised in Southern California. She started learning the clarinet when she was nine years old and still loves to play in her free time. Andrea began writing in middle school and has never stopped coming up with new ideas for stories or poems. Her creativity has driven her to discover more about the world for inspiration. She has traveled to over sixteen countries, mostly for her studies, and draws inspiration from the people she has met and the places she has visited.